ECHOES

OF THE

GREAT EXHIBITION.

Hears not also mortal life
. . . .
Voices? . . . . WORDSWORTH.

Not by might, nor by power, but by my spirit, saith the Lord of hosts. ZECH. IV. 6.

BY JOSEPH TURNER.

LONDON:
WILLIAM PICKERING
1851.

In the interest of creating a more extensive selection of rare historical book reprints, we have chosen to reproduce this title even though it may possibly have occasional imperfections such as missing and blurred pages, missing text, poor pictures, markings, dark backgrounds and other reproduction issues beyond our control. Because this work is culturally important, we have made it available as a part of our commitment to protecting, preserving and promoting the world's literature. Thank you for your understanding.

I.

Them that honour Me, I will honour, but they that despise Me shall be lightly esteemed. 1 Sam. ii. 30.

GLORY to God, from whom this thought descended,
    And by whose grace 'tis perfected in act!
Glory to Him, whose mighty arm extended
Hath wrought in Britain's isle this wondrous fact!
To Him, whose grace His word to us hath given!
To Him, who here that word hath glorified!
Through Whom, no rent our robe of peace hath riven
When all earth's kingdoms were with shakings tried.
Hence are we set on high amid the nations,
To us they trust their best and brightest things,—
Hence to us standing on the sure foundations
Free Truth, free Thought, free Word, such glory clings;
Nor shall we slip from such high elevations,
Till God, dishonour'd, low our glory brings!

II.

On the First of May, 1851, the opening Day of the Exhibition.

FITLY hath this May dawn as May arisen,
   May of the brightest promise earth hath seen,
Since from the Olives He who broke death's prison
Rose as Heaven's pledge of Peace to earth's terrene.
Fruit of that peace, the nations' peace with nations
The clarions' clamour doth this morn proclaim,
Whose heralds here, in order's seemly stations
Meet round Victoria's throne in Peace's name.
First fruit of peace on Earth! O well may quiver
Her Albert's lip with humbly conscious pride,
And his heart throb its thanks to Peace's Giver,
While to this hall he sees in rushing tide
Concordant Nations flow as a full river!

III.

To the Queen.

By Me kings reign, and princes decree justice.
Rom. viii. 15.

BLEST be the hand that wields the staff of rule
   So nobly over England and her world
Of infant Empires, learners in her school
Of Freedom, Truth, and Right, where'er unfurled
Her flag hath spread its triple sign of Peace,
Love, and good-will to man.   Blest by best grace
Of Him who raiseth and who ruleth kings
Be that Queen's heart, whose glory loudest rings
As nursing mother of all good and beauteous
To her own realm, and *here,* to all the earth,
Whose Universe of nations, here the duteous
Tribute of honour yieldeth to her worth.
Blest be Victoria! may her offspring studious
Of her example, reign with right above their birth!

IV.

TO THE PRINCE ALBERT.

Then they that be wise shall shine as the brightness of the firmament. DANIEL xii. 3.

HAIL to the prince thro' whom this Day-star rose!
Thro' whose continuous care it culminated,
Who by no empty vanity inflated
Willed it should prosper, spite of fearful foes
To his great aim, that all men should inherit
Unfading blessings thro' the might of Peace,
And mutual helpfulness of labour's merit
Thro' God's good-will, and unrespective grace.
Hail to the prince who so hath been ensample
How great ones of the earth should fraternize
In glorious purposed toil, nor lose their ample
Income, of blessing by self-sacrifice.
Hail to that prince. His fame no time shall trample
But with th' Eternal Host his star shall rise!

V.

To the Exhibitors.

In all labour there is profit. PROV. xiv. 23.

HAIL ye who sent this Glory's glories here!
   Who spared not of your Best, to eternize
This Wonder's fame to earth's most distant year,
   And blend your several lights into the rise
Of a new morning star upon the nations,
   Whose light shall gladden their expectant eyes,
And ripen fruits of Union's federations
   Thro' Peace and Industry's firm wedlock ties.
Sure is your guerdon, profit sure of labour.
   In blessing hath the Maker set the rule
Of toil for mutual good to every neighbour
   And brother of one blood, in this life's school
Of hearts for blessed love. Thro' whom the tabor
Of conquering Peace shall yet confound the war-
     ring Fool.

VI.

To the Royal Commission.

I will not give my glory to another, nor my praise to graven images. ISAI. xlii. 8.

THANKS unto all who have this nursling tended
From the seed germ up to the stately tree,
Great Banian to the growths of mind that blended
Beneath its shade their subtle tracery.
Thanks to them all. Tho' human failure mingled
With their good effort, great the total sum
Of rich Inheritance for earth to come.
One error from the heap must yet be singled,
Which still may flourish forth with evil fruit.
God's message to the Universe unplacèd
In highest room, tho' England's pride and root
Of her great name. For holy things debasèd
(Thro' the good Giver's jealous attribute,)
She yet may see her pride with shame disgracèd.

VII.

TO THE ASSEMBLED NATIONS.

Blessed are the peacemakers, for they shall be called the children of God. MATT. v. 9.

HAIL to the Tribes who here have been assembled!
To the confederate Nations health and peace!
At their close union well may those have trembled
Who would not that doomed war thro' earth should cease.
Hail to those tribes who here have been united
By the strong ties of common aim and weal;
By no harsh jarrings be that welfare blighted,
May their hosts ne'er uplift for strife the steel!
Hail to the tribes who England's call have heeded,
Who mixed their voices with her loud acclaim
That the fair light of truth must not be shaded
If they would touch the zenith of true fame.
All they who here her strife for Peace have aided,
We hail with the Peacemakers' blessed name!

VIII.

REFLECTIONS ON THOSE ASSEMBLED.

Strive to enter in at the strait gate, for many, I say unto you, shall seek to enter in, and shall not *be able.* LUKE xiii. 24.

WHAT myriad glories of th' imàge divine,
    What myriad of the human, hère have been
Gathered, and severed? When, to meet again?
For ah! the undeveloped beauty-line
Of reborn spirit, could in few be tracèd;—
And shall such worlds of Dignity disgracèd
From its high birthright, share indeed the doom
Of all that is not Heaven? Tho' deepest gloom
For us hang o'er their future, we yet know
Love hath once said, "The strait gate strive to enter,
The Many still 'long Hell's broad pathway go,
Upon that flowery steep do Thou not venture,
And see Thou rescue all Thou canst from woe."
O would that all would seek health from their sins'
       calènture.

IX.

Reflections continued.

Sin entered into the world, and Death by sin, . . . for that *all* have sinned. Rom. v. 12.

THIS world is cursed.—Its beauty shall be marred.—
Such Truth's sad response given to the asking
Where sink the Lovely? Multitudes illstarred
With fairest form, and in hope's sunshine basking,
Shall yet be fled from as accursed things,
Foul graves of love, where Hell's dread death-bell rings,
Blasted by glare of Evil admiration.
Units alone, who scape that fell temptation
Thro' timely heed, or scorn of aught but good,
Shall their sweet souls from agony deliver
And join the ever lovely angel-brood.
Some after woeful fall, the gracious Giver
Of life to lost ones, shall with heavenly food
Revive, and wash in Christ's stain cleansing river.

X.

THE EXHIBITION, VIEWED AS A STEP IN THE MANIFESTED AND DESIGNED PROGRESS OF THE HUMAN RACE.

Ye shall be as Gods, knowing good and evil. GEN. iii. 5.

SO spake the glozing tempter, false, yet true.
   False in *his* meaning, true, in the divine.
Low as himself, he would that they should rue,
God from that Foul, to gods will them refine.
Unwittingly the Liar did fore-tell
   Most godlike Truth, in words that came from hell;
But glory to the love divine doth cling,
   From Evil, Good, from Falsehood, Truth to bring.
So Satan vanquished is by his own ill,
So are his victims robèd with a Light
Brighter than all his fears: so lives he still,
But as a witness for that love and right
Which he would frustrate, so his subtlest skill
Hath wrought but for himself, sorer satanic blight.

XI.

WARNING AGAINST BEING DAZZLED BY THE GLORIES OF THIS WORLD AROUND, HERE COLLECTED.

To him that overcometh, will I give to sit with Me upon my throne, even as I also overcame, and am set down with my Father upon His throne. REV. iii. 21.

HIGHER and higher still, *my* soul, aspire!
   Seize thy new heirship, soar above the spheres!
There be thou borne on wings of rapid years,
Not 'neath the Judge's throne content to tire,
But with Him thereon placed, to overcome.
All finite glory's lesser summits' doom
Thence clear behold thou, rest not lower down
Than His great Voice hath called thee—not alone,
But *all* the victors over flesh and evil.
So rule thou here thine own Dust's meaner kind,
So trample each vain gaud of world or devil,
So share that Victor's self-devoting mind,
So reign o'er nations of a lower level!

XII.

WARNING AGAINST MISTAKING THE MEANING OF THE WRITER.

There shall be upon the Earth distress of nations, with perplexity. . . . . . . The powers of Heaven shall be shaken.
LUKE xxi. 25. 26.

ERR not, ye peoples, tho' we sing this glory—
'Tis not *this* way earth's final bliss shall come.
Of judgment ere that peace, prophetic story
Doth sure foreshow, and the swift nearing doom
Of all who seek mere earthly aggrandation
Of wealth or honour, mindless of the One
From whom comes all true merit and renown.
'Tis as a gage of higher elevation
We celebrate this fading Glory's fame;
What *could* be, were all men in federation
To work as fellow-helpers in His name.
While then ye toil in love's co-operation
See that ye earn not their lasting shame,
Who the great Donor still forget in the donation!

XIII.

ON THE LAST PUBLIC WEEK AND DAY OF THE EXHIBITION.

NOW the last hour draws nigh of growing Wonder,
Well may men crowd to chant its sad farewell!
Well may the ocean-rush and trampling thunder
Of hurrying hosts its rapid doom foretell!
The sadness at their hearts doth on them hasten!
More of such glory would they, ere no more
It bless their sight, well may such sadness chasten
The joy they walked in 'mid those treasures' store.
The hour hath come of trembling expectation—
The flutter of their hearts is as a bird
In th' eager silence. Ah! with its last vibration
The fountain's jet of life the air hath stirred.
Oh! with what burst of thankful exultation
Their hearts' high voice in song and shouts is heard.

XIV.

The Night of the public Closing.

AND now the last are gone of lingering lovers.
Ichăbōd here is writ on glory's reign.
Guards and the silent statues are the movers
Of echoes here, ne'er to resound again
With hum of hosts, concordant in their wonder.
Better King Godfrey's ears had heard such thunder
Than his Cross-bearers shouting in their Pride
War for that cross! By peace, *here* glorified!
Now ruleth here his image 'mid such still
And spectral shapes, 'neath this dim canopy
As bear our phantasy amid those chill
Inheritors of death's pale panoply,
Whose fame did once Earth's space with echoes fill,
Now statued in her Hall of History.

XV.

ON THE WANT OF A PUBLIC THANKSGIVING CLOSE, ANSWERING TO THE PUBLIC PRAYER OPENING.

There have not returned to give glory to God, save this stranger. LUKE xvii. 18.

WAS it a top-stone to the witness-heap
    Even *here* to add, that human good must fail,
Her fairest promise drag a scaly tail
Of unperformance; that *we* could not keep
Our promises of praise for granted prayer?
A pillar to our shame 'fore total earth to rear!
Alas! poor England! must her great ones still
The longings of her true sons unfulfil,
And their own noblest gages fail to keep
For their weak heart! The people's, *it* was strong,
They would not to themselves do the foul wrong
Of public thanklessness. All hearts *did* leap—
All voices would have swell'd the full Hosanna Song
To Him who did His own prayer-hearing promise
    keep!

XVI.

Consolation on the Closing.

Cast thy bread upon the waters, for thou shalt find it after many days. Eccl. xi. 1.

THIS Glory hath been, not to be again!
   Such the dread sentence writ on earthly glory.
Yet may we cheer our sadness with the story
Of life resurgent, Profit born of Pain.
For such the gracious law of the All-loving,
The harvest springeth from the seed that dies,—
So may we safely trust that He approving
Much fruit shall from this fallen Glory rise.
Since from Light's Author we this Light have seen,
So may we our sad Hearts from grief deliver
While closing even such a Glory's e'en.
So trust we sure that an o'erflowing River
Of Blessing shall the watered Nations green
From wide sown Seeds of fruitful Labour's sheen.

XVII.

ON THE TRUE GREATNESS OF THIS GLORY.

HERE hath earth's wiser latter day beheld
   Her last most wondrous Wonder. Here she saw
Her millions flock in Peace and under law
Of mutual Love; of glories which this palace fill'd
They in their Harmony the greatest glory.
For of the world's wild youth the constant story
Tells that such Hosts met but for Wrath and Blood.
But here the Nations' bannered Brotherhood
With one heart waved their witness unto Heaven,
That here their minds' fine issues came as leaven
To work their masses' thought unto a food
Of fuller life to all of Adam's blood.
To Britain hath her God such favour given,
   That on her soil hath first so great a Glory stood.

XVIII.

On seeing a great Bible open in the Exhibition at the following Prophecy.

> Behold, He cometh with clouds, and every eye shall see Him, and they also which pierced Him, and all kindreds of the Earth shall wail because of Him. Rev. i. 7.

PATENT to all the gathered Nations' eyes
   (Was it yet lookèd on by aught but mine?)
The Book held forth this solemn warning line,
Sure gage of glory to the timely Wise
Lookers for Him, the centre of their souls,
The Sun of all their love-attracted spheres.
But for unwatchful virgins, it but rolls
Dread thunder peals of conscience dooming fears.
Of that wide World, for whom beneath this roof
That awful bell its deep-toned summons knelled,
How many of such test would stand the proof
Were lightnings of His Advent then beheld?
Shall Froth upon Time's wave still hold aloof
Hearts, for whose love and life His life outwelled?

Printed by Libri Plureos GmbH in Hamburg, Germany